For the *Love* of NASCAR

An A-to-Z Primer for NASCAR Fans of All Ages

Written by Michael Fresina and the publishers of *NASCAR Scene*
Illustrated by Mark Anderson

"TO SAY THAT NASCAR HAS BEEN A BIG PART OF MY LIFE, AND THE LIVES OF MY ENTIRE FAMILY, IS A HUGE UNDERSTATEMENT."

The King

Starting with my daddy Lee, myself, my brother Maurice, my wife Lynda, my cousin Dale Inman, my son Kyle, my other wonderful children and grandchildren—excuse me, but I hope you get the idea—we've been a part of NASCAR almost from the day of its existence.

We've seen the sport grow from its grassroots days when it was little more than a regional sport to the vastly popular entity it is today. I have to be honest: when I was a young man trying to follow in my father's footsteps as a multiple NASCAR champion, I never could have imagined the sport would be what it is now.

I am very proud that my family has played a significant role in all of it.

NASCAR's growth has brought with it plenty of new products for the fans' enjoyment, not the least of which have been books—some of which have been about me, and I'm pleased about that.

But this one isn't about me. It's about NASCAR, but in a way never before presented. It's simple, entertaining, and downright fun for fans of all ages.

For the Love of NASCAR: An A-to-Z Primer for NASCAR Fans of All Ages is a terrific way to learn something about the sport, what it is, and the people who helped to make it so. It's not deep, it's not detailed, but it is fun. To me, that's what matters most. And I promise you that you will learn something and perhaps be enticed to discover even more.

This book is about entertainment and education for everyone. I'm especially pleased that it will become a part of the library at the Victory Junction Gang camp. Now, I have to tell you something. I really like the letter "P." Check it out.

The Petty family says to you: enjoy!

—Richard Petty

"A" is for American,

Like fresh apple pie.
NASCAR's appeal
You cannot deny.

"B" is for Bristol,

A favorite among tracks,
And on its high banks
Drivers must watch their backs.

BRISTOL MOTOR SPEEDWAY, located in Bristol, Tennessee, is the second shortest track on the Nextel Cup circuit. A .533-mile oval, Bristol is a fan favorite for its tight quarters and 36-degree banked turns—the steepest on the current Nextel Cup schedule.

The track has played host to some of the most dramatic, collision-riddled events in stock car history. Two of the sport's most notorious bump-and-run incidents took place at Bristol—and involved the same two drivers! On August 26, 1995, Dale Earnhardt and Terry Labonte were battling for the win on the final lap of the Goody's 500. Labonte was able to hold Earnhardt off as the two began a sprint to the finish. Earnhardt, in a controversial move, "bumped" Labonte and sent him spinning—right across the finish line! Four years later an identical duel ensued. This time Earnhardt's "bump" was more effective, and he was able to slide past the spinning Labonte for the win.

"C" is for Charlotte,

Where racing is king
And checkered flag thrills
Are a commonplace thing.

DAYTONA MAY BE NASCAR'S OFFICIAL HOME, but North Carolina's Queen City sits undeniably at racing's epicenter. Lowe's Motor Speedway, a 1.5-mile superspeedway, opened in 1960. It plays host to the Coca-Cola 600 every spring, the UAW-GM 500 in the fall, and has been home to 19 of the first 20 all-star races.

Some of stock car racing's most memorable moments took place in Charlotte, including Dale Earnhardt's 1987 "Pass in the Grass." In the 1992 all-star race, Davey Allison won traveling sideways, and then crashed, in one of the wildest finishes in NASCAR history. Allison had to be told that he'd won the race in the Infield Care Center before being transported to the hospital.

Today more than a dozen race teams are based in the Charlotte region. Hendrick Motorsports, Dale Earnhardt Inc., Richard Childress Racing, Joe Gibbs Racing, Chip Ganassi Racing, Evernham Motorsports, Roush Racing, and Penske Racing all call the area home.

"D" is for Daytona,

NASCAR's most famous site,
Where a win is the goal
And the racing is tight.

BEFORE DAYTONA INTERNATIONAL SPEEDWAY WAS BUILT IN 1959, Daytona Beach was the site of early stock car races. Cars would kick up the sand in races scheduled to coincide with low tide. When the speedway was finished, it immediately became the crown jewel of the NASCAR circuit. A full 2.5-mile superspeedway, the new site hosted its first 500-mile race on February 22, 1959. Daytona's high-banked turns were initially received with mixed reviews for encouraging average lap speeds exceeding 200 mph. When asked why he chose 31-degree banks, NASCAR founder Bill France said, "Because they couldn't lay asphalt any steeper."

A victory in the Daytona 500 is the holy grail for NASCAR drivers and teams. It's put names like Greg Sacks and Derrike Cope on the map. And for those who chase the grail for years before finding satisfaction—like Dale Earnhardt and Darrell Waltrip—the first Daytona 500 victory is the sweetest reward.

"E" will always be Earnhardt—

The Intimidator and Man in Black. With three fingers held high He's remembered at every track.

DALE EARNHARDT WAS BORN TO RACE—AND WIN. Son of dirt-track legend Ralph Earnhardt, the child who would become the Intimidator was behind the wheel as soon as his feet could reach the pedals. Once on the NASCAR Cup circuit, Earnhardt ruffled the feathers—and dented the bumpers—of more than a few racing veterans caught off guard by his aggressive style and frequent success. Before his tragic death on the final lap of the 2001 Daytona 500, Earnhardt won seven Cup championships, recorded 76 career Cup wins, took home four IROC championships, and was the most loved—and despised—man at every track on the circuit. His legion of followers plastered their vehicles with Earnhardt stickers and greeted each other with a familiar three-fingered wave. Fans troubled by his aggressive style and jealous of his success were equally passionate in their criticism of the Man in Black.

"F" is for France,

NASCAR's famous first clan.
They created a sport
To excite every fan.

AFTER YEARS OF PROMOTING RACES ON THE SANDS OF DAYTONA and trying to establish a national championship race, Bill France gathered promoters from around the Southeast for a meeting in 1947. His goals were simple: to establish a governing body to regulate stock car racing, to create rules to keep cars mechanically uniform, and to develop a point system that would allow drivers to vie for a national championship. On February 21, 1948, the National Association for Stock Car Automobile Racing was born.

In 1972 Bill France passed the role of president and CEO of NASCAR on to his son, William C. France, widely known as Bill France Jr., who guided the sport until the end of the 2000 season and is largely credited with its meteoric rise in popularity during the nineties.

Today the France family still occupies more than half the seats on NASCAR's board of directors.

"G" is for Gordon,

Golden boy from out West. He owns four Winston Cups And is one of the best.

JEFF GORDON, NOW A MEMBER OF NASCAR'S INNER CIRCLE, did not make it to the top by way of Tobacco Road. In a sport long dominated by good ol' Southern boys, Gordon's California pedigree and squeaky-clean image didn't endear him to many hardcore fans—initially.

It seems, however, that Gordon was destined for Cup greatness. In 1993 he was the circuit's Rookie of the Year. In 1994 he won his first race, and in 1995 he won his first of four Cup titles.

Gordon's popularity has transcended the sport. He is the only NASCAR driver to have hosted *Saturday Night Live* and frequently subs as host on the *Live with Regis and Kelly* show. In 2004 Gordon made it to the finals of Bravo's immensely popular *Celebrity Poker Showdown*. But even though his interests have broadened, his focus is still on racing, as both a partial team owner and an ultracompetitive driver.

"H" is for horsepower.

It's the goal every week.
Day and night in the shop
The engines they tweak.

"I" is for Indy,

Where racing gained fame.
Once NASCAR arrived
It was never the same.

INDIANAPOLIS MOTOR SPEEDWAY, better known as the Brickyard, has played host to "the Greatest Spectacle in Racing"—the Indianapolis 500—since 1911, and first welcomed stock car racing to the track in 1994. Built in 1909 using 3.2 million bricks (the only remaining sign of which is the start/finish line), the 2.5-mile rectangular track was designed for open-wheel racing. It took NASCAR 50 years to establish a degree of credibility and popularity significant enough for IMS to embrace a NASCAR event.

On August 6, 1994, the NASCAR Nation descended upon Indy's sacred ground for the inaugural Brickyard 400. On that day, local favorite Jeff Gordon took the checkered flag and NASCAR's first sip of Indy's celebratory bottle of milk. NASCAR has been back to Indy every year since. Jeff Gordon continues to shine, having won four times, each in front of nearly three hundred thousand fans.

"J" is for Junior—

Dale's son has the name,
But by his own skill
May exceed his dad's fame.

DALE EARNHARDT JR. NEVER DENIED HIS LEGENDARY ROOTS. The youngest son of Dale Earnhardt, Junior is following in his father's famous footsteps. After fulfilling his father's wishes and graduating from high school in 1992, Junior worked for two years as a junior mechanic at his father's Chevrolet dealership. In 1994 he shared his desire to race with his famous family. By 1998 he was racing full time on the Busch series and won the championship—a feat repeated in 1999. That same year he inked a deal with Budweiser to begin racing on the Cup circuit for his father's team. By 2000 Junior was running the entire Cup schedule and had made the big time.

In less than five years of Cup racing, Junior has won more than a dozen races and is the unofficial poster boy for NASCAR's next generation.

"K" is for Kenseth,

Who took Winston's last throne.
His next title will come
With a free Nextel phone.

MATT KENSETH WON THE NASCAR CHAMPIONSHIP IN 2003, Winston's final season as the sport's title sponsor. Recording one of the most consistent season-long efforts in racing history, Kenseth took the title despite winning just one race. His 11 top-five and series-high 25 top-ten finishes were enough to secure NASCAR's most coveted prize and close the Winston era.

Kenseth is a relative newcomer to NASCAR, having posted his first full season of Cup competition in 2000. With the support of team owner and racing legend Jack Roush, Kenseth is poised to build on his success in the Nextel era.

"L" is for

Labonte,

Brothers Terry and Bobby. With three champions' titles, Racing's more than a hobby.

THE LABONTE BROTHERS share more than just deep Texas roots and a passion for driving: they are the only siblings in NASCAR history to share multiple Cup series' championships. Terry, eight years his brother's senior, has won two Cup titles (1984 and 1996) in his quarter-century career and has earned more than $35 million. Bobby, whose career winnings also top $35 million, had a humble start in the sport, sweeping the floors for Terry's team at Hagan Racing in 1982. By 1993 he was racing full time on the Cup circuit, and in 2000 he won a championship of his own.

"M" is for Mark Martin,

Four times second best. Winning a title Is his final quest.

A NATIVE OF BATESVILLE, ARKANSAS, MARK MARTIN began his stock car racing career at age 15 and notched his first-ever victory at a local track in 1974 in just his third start. By 1981 he was ready to roll with the big boys and entered five NASCAR Cup races as an independent driver/owner. Running a full schedule in 1982, he recorded eight top 10s and finished second to Geoffrey Bodine for Rookie of the Year honors. From 1989–2000 he was among the top 10 in championship points every season and finished second in the Cup chase four times (1990, 1994, 1998, and 2002). His strongest effort came in 1998, when he won a career-best seven races, including the inaugural event at Las Vegas Motor Speedway, but finished behind Jeff Gordon in the title chase. As his career winds down, Martin's singular focus is winning a Cup championship.

"N" is for NASCAR,

Where they work without rest
And listen to fans
To make their sport the best.

INCORPORATED ON FEBRUARY 21, 1948, the National Association for Stock Car Auto Racing is the sanctioning body for the premier stock car racing circuits in the world. NASCAR operates three national series: the NASCAR Nextel Cup Series, the NASCAR Busch Series, and the NASCAR Craftsman Truck Series.

One of NASCAR's chief responsibilities is maintaining fair and equal competition. The organization must generate and enforce rules regarding car and engine specifications, driver safety, and driver and team conduct on the track and in the pit area. As the stakes get higher with prize money and exposure at an all-time high, monitoring driver conduct and penalizing recklessness has become a full-time job for NASCAR.

"O" is for the ovals

Where legends take flight.
In steel rockets on wheels,
They never turn right.

"P" is for Petty,

A family of champs.
They're more than just drivers—
For charity, they host camps.

Adam Petty

A FARMER BY TRADE, LEE PETTY turned his attention to stock car racing after the Great Depression decimated much of the agricultural industry. Renowned for doing anything to win, he once attached armor plating and wing nuts to the side of his Oldsmobile so that when his car brushed against another, his opponent's sheet metal would be shredded.

Son Richard Petty was born in 1937 and by 1958 was racing full time. Before long, he was well on his way to becoming "the King." By the end of his career he had won seven Cup championships and two hundred races. Richard's son, Kyle, upheld the family racing tradition as the King's career wound to an end in 1992. Kyle began racing in 1979, but is best known as a savvy businessman and community leader.

IN 2000 KYLE'S SON ADAM became the first fourth-generation driver to compete at his sport's highest level. Although he had a promising future and a legendary pedigree, Adam died tragically following a wreck in practice at New Hampshire International Speedway on May 12, 2000.

The Petty family's vision for a camp to enrich the lives of children suffering chronic and/or life-threatening illnesses took shape in June 2004. The Victory Junction Gang Camp is the passion of Kyle Petty and his wife, Pattie.

"Q" is for qualifying.

A shot at the pole
      Is each driver's dream
And every team's goal.

"R" is for
race fans,
Thrilled by roaring cars.
They cheer every lap
And enjoy drivers' wars.

THE ROUGHLY 75 MILLION NASCAR FANS are among the most loyal and devoted in all of sports. Arriving in droves to support their favorite drivers, they turn weekends at the track into three-day festivals of fun and frivolity. Each year more than 6 million people attend NASCAR Cup races. Several races draw crowds that exceed the attendance at the Super Bowl, a World Series game, and an NBA Finals game *combined*. NASCAR fans wear their devotion on hats, shirts, bumper stickers and even on caskets and limited-edition automobiles. In 2003 fans purchased more than $2 billion in NASCAR-licensed products. No longer a regional passion, NASCAR is an international phenomenon, drawing more than 50 percent of its fans from outside the Southern states and from as far away as New Zealand and Asia.

"S" is for sponsors,

Whose support and hard cash
Make racing and titles
A yearlong mad dash.

NASCAR IS NOT FUELED BY HIGH-OCTANE PETROLEUM OR THE LOYALTY OF ITS FANS ALONE. More than 900 companies hold some form of NASCAR sponsorship, accounting for approximately $400 million in involvement each year. Nextel's 10-year title sponsorship agreement has a value of $750 million. Without the "fuel" sponsors provide, NASCAR couldn't deliver the best in sports and entertainment.

"T" is for Tony.

On the track he's not kind. And because of his style He often gets fined.

WINNING TITLES AT THE CUP LEVEL, in the Indy Racing League, and as a driver in the United States Auto Club, Tony Stewart's success is without equal. He has finished among the top 10 in NASCAR Cup championship points every year since he joined the circuit. One would think his popularity would be as unquestioned as his drive to win, but it is not—unless one considers incurring the wrath of fans, officials, and competitors popularity.

Stewart has been fined more than $100,000 for incidents ranging from on-track recklessness to assaulting a photographer. His aggressive, take-no-prisoners style appeals to a lot of fans, but leaves others angry as their favorite drivers are pushed to the back of the pack. Driving as a member of the Joe Gibbs Racing family and under contract through 2009, Stewart's success and antics are sure to continue well into the future.

"U" is the underdog

Who surprises the field And wins a lone title By refusing to yield.

ALAN KULWICKI IS NASCAR'S ALL-TIME FAVORITE UNDERDOG. At a time when multicar teams were beginning to form small racing conglomerates and independent driver/owners were nearing extinction, Kulwicki burst on the Cup scene in 1985 with a used car and just two crew members. By 1990 he had recorded nine top-10 finishes and was offered $1 million to race for Junior Johnson. Kulwicki— ever the independent—turned down the offer.

In the final race of the 1992 season in Atlanta, Kulwicki was within striking distance of a Cup championship. Bill Elliott won the race but finished second in the points chase to Kulwicki, who triumphed by leading just one more lap than Elliott. Kulwicki celebrated his title the same way he did each of his wins: with a "Polish Victory Lap," traveling in the wrong direction, waving to the frenzied crowd.

Kulwicki's time in the sun was short-lived, however. One of the perks of winning the title was the use of his sponsor's private plane. That plane, bound for Bristol, Tennessee, on April 1, 1993, crashed mysteriously, killing Kulwicki and three others on board.

"V" is for victory lane,

Where traditions unfold:
The "hat dance" for photos
And a "beer shower" so cold.

THE GOAL FOR EVERY RACE TEAM is to end the day in victory lane, which is actually a circle, not a lane. It is there that they receive their giant cardboard checks and ostentatious trophies. More than a place to be dubbed "King for a Day," victory lane has become a place of both mad celebrations and corporate obligations.

After plowing through traffic at dizzying speed for several hours and finishing on top, drivers emerge from red-hot stock cars and proceed to drink, throw, and spray liquids ranging from water and soda to champagne and beer. After things settle down a bit, interviews are conducted and then there is the "hat dance," the ultimate in choreographed chaos. As the team tries to contain its elation and pose for pictures with the car, trophy, and winner's check, a swarm of marketing and promotions personnel hover around handing hats to each member of the team. Each hat bears the logo of one of the team's various corporate sponsors—and of course each sponsor expects a picture of the winning team, wearing its hat, in victory lane.

"W" is for Waltrips,

Racing's famed pair.
One races for wins;
One calls them on air.

MICHAEL AND OLDER BROTHER DARRELL WALTRIP hail from Owensboro, Kentucky. Today, Michael is an active driver on both the Busch and Nextel Cup circuits. Darrell, now retired from the track except for an occasional run in the Craftsman Truck Series, has taken a spot in the broadcast booth for Fox Television.

Darrell, known to many current race fans as the boisterous guy who announces the start of each race with his now-famous "Boogity, Boogity, Boogity" line, is a three-time Cup champion (1981, 1982, and 1985) and one of racing's most legendary drivers. He began racing karts at age 12. By the time he was a teenager, he had moved on to larger vehicles and was even arrested for attempted drag racing, had his driver's license suspended, and was forced to ride a moped for a year.

Michael didn't rush into a life in racing, waiting until 1986 to begin a full-time Cup career. He holds the record for the longest active streak of Cup races *without* a victory: 463. He ended the streak in the 2001 Daytona 500, but his triumph was overshadowed by the tragic death of his team owner, Dale Earnhardt, in a crash on the race's final lap.

"X" is for extreme.

These guys like to trade paint.
What's normal in NASCAR
Might make others feel faint.

"Y" is for the young guns.

They are racing's new breed. Fame and fortune they like, But what they need is more speed.

A NEW GENERATION OF DRIVERS has emerged on the Nextel Cup circuit. Branded "young guns," these 20-somethings stormed onto the scene and forced racing's old guard to sit up and take notice. Aggressive, brash, and bold, the young guns are unwilling to simply bide their time, take their knocks, and learn from the back of the pack. This new breed has kicked down the door and stormed to the top of the standings. Dale Earnhardt Jr., Tony Stewart, Ryan Newman, Matt Kenseth, Kurt Busch, Jamie McMurray, Kevin Harvick, Jimmie Johnson, and Casey Kahne are just a few of the young guns poised to take NASCAR to a new generation of fans.

"Z" is for zoom

It's the sound the cars make
Speeding around the track
With records to break.

On May 5, 1997, Mark Martin recorded **THE FASTEST AVERAGE SPEED** in a championship points race when he scorched Talladega Superspeedway with a blistering 188.354-mph average.

The fastest lap times in NASCAR history took place in qualifying rounds. With the track to themselves and a car set up for maximum power for a short time, drivers let it all hang out. The fastest single-lap qualifying time in NASCAR history was recorded by Bill Elliott, who posted a lap speed of 212.809 mph at Talladega Superspeedway on April 30, 1987. After NASCAR mandated the use of restrictor plates (thin aluminum plates that restrict airflow from the carburetor to the engine and reduce horsepower) at Daytona and Talladega in 1989, the fastest qualifying lap was run by Elliott at 199.388 mph in 1990. As long as restrictor-plate racing is the standard at the circuit's two fastest tracks, Elliot's 212.809 will stand unsurpassed.

"A" is for **America**

"B" is for **Bristol**

"D" is for **Daytona**

"E" is for **Earnhardt**

"G" is for **Gordon**

"J" is for **Junior**

"K" is for **Kenseth**

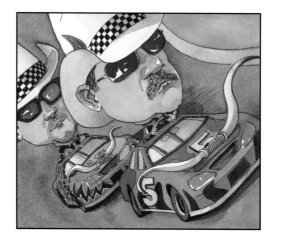

"L" is for **Labonte**

"M" is for **Martin**

"O" is for **Oval**

"P" is for **Petty**

"T" is for **Tony**

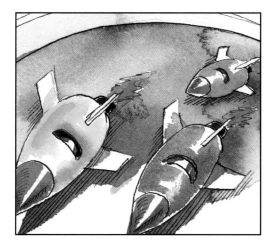

"W" is for **Waltrip**

"X" is for **eXtreme**

"A" is for **Artist**

"W" is for Writer

Library of Congress Control Number: 2004114944

This book is available in quantity at special discounts for your group or organization.
For further information, contact:

Triumph Books
601 South LaSalle St.
Suite 500
Chicago, Illinois 60605
312-939-3330
Fax 312-663-3557

Printed in U.S.A.
ISBN 1-57243-732-4